# HOW STORIES CAME INTO THE WORLD

A Folk Tale from West Africa

*Retold and illustrated by*

## Joanna Troughton

**Blackie**
London

**Bedrick/Blackie**
New York

Mouse goes everywhere. Through rich and poor men's houses she creeps. All night with her bright little eyes she watches the doing of secret things, and no treasure chamber is so safe but she can tunnel through and see what is hidden there.

In the olden days Mouse wove a story picture from all that she saw, and to each she gave different colours. The stories became her children and lived with her because Mouse had no children of her own.

This is the first of Mouse's stories . . .

Many years ago Sun and Moon were great friends and lived on earth together. Sun often visited his friend the Water, but Water never returned his visits.

One day Sun asked Water, 'Why do you never visit me?'

Water replied, 'Your house isn't big enough. If you wish me to visit, you must build a very large compound. It must be very big as my people take up a lot of room.'

So Sun and Moon built a very large compound and when it was finished they invited Water and his people to visit them.

When Water arrived he called out, 'Is it safe for us to enter?'

'Yes, come in,' said Sun.

So Water and his people began to flow in.

'Is it still safe?' asked Water.

'Yes,' said Sun.

So more and more water flowed in, and it became deeper and deeper.

Soon it became so deep that Sun and Moon had to perch on the roof of their house.

'Is it still safe?' asked Water.

'Yes,' said Sun.

So Water overflowed the top of the roof and Sun and Moon were forced to go up into the sky where they have stayed ever since.

Long ago the Earth God asked the Sky God and all his people to a great feast. In those times all the animals lived in the sky – so they were the Sky God's people. Now, the day before the feast the Earth God ordered every tree and bush to bring forth plenty of ripe and juicy fruit. When the animals arrived on earth with their master, they saw all the good things to eat and they spread out all over the land and began feeding.

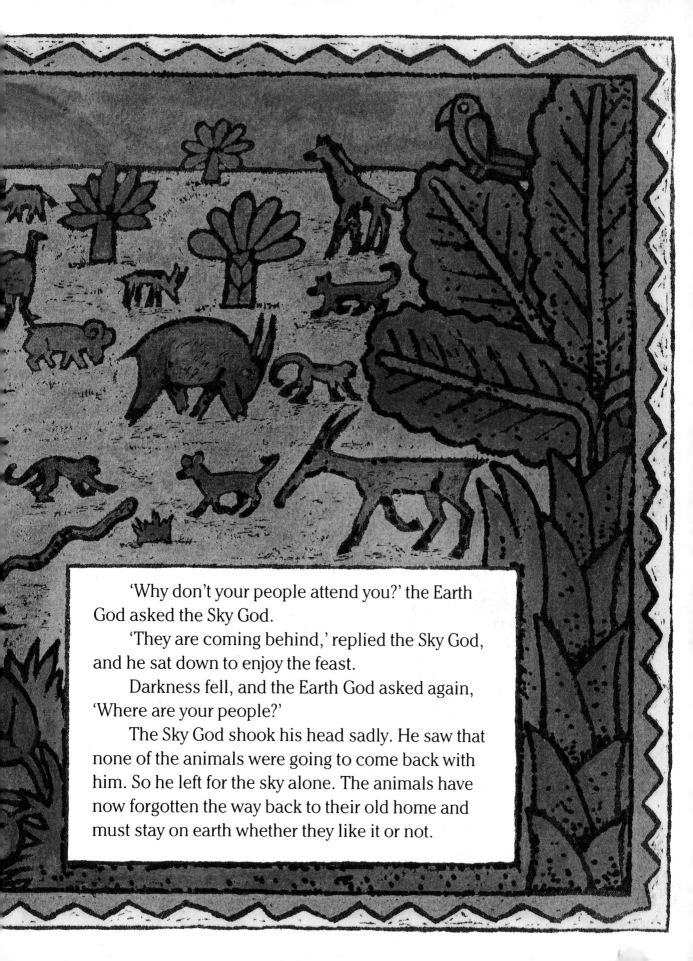

'Why don't your people attend you?' the Earth God asked the Sky God.

'They are coming behind,' replied the Sky God, and he sat down to enjoy the feast.

Darkness fell, and the Earth God asked again, 'Where are your people?'

The Sky God shook his head sadly. He saw that none of the animals were going to come back with him. So he left for the sky alone. The animals have now forgotten the way back to their old home and must stay on earth whether they like it or not.

There was once a drought in the land so the animals decided to dig a well. Everyone worked very hard – except Hare. He was lazy, so he hid until all the work had been done. When the well was finished, Hare took a calabash and beat it loudly with a stick. It made such a noise that the animals took fright and ran away.

Hare came out of his hiding place and drank his fill at the new well. Then he washed himself and made the water dirty. When the animals returned they saw the muddy water and knew they had been tricked. 'We shall set a trap,' they said. So they made a rubber girl out of the sticky resin of the rubber tree, and placed the girl by the well.

The next day Hare came once more to drink at the well. He saw the rubber girl standing there and thought she was real. 'Hallo,' he said. But the rubber girl didn't reply, and Hare's paw had stuck fast. He tried to pull himself free but the more he struggled the more he stuck. When the animals arrived they knew Hare was their thief. 'Go away from the bush,' they told him. 'And never return.'

They pulled Hare free from the rubber girl and drove him away to the grasslands. And he is still there to this day.

Many years ago the Hippopotamus invited all the animals to a great feast. But just as everyone was about to begin eating the Hippo said, 'You have come to feed at my table but none of you know my name. You cannot eat my food until you know my name.'

Now the Hippo's name was a well kept secret, so the animals had to go hungry.

Then Tortoise said, 'What would you do if I discovered your name?'

Hippo replied, 'I would be so ashamed that my whole family and I would leave the land and go and dwell in the water forever.'

'I will discover your name by the time of the next feast,' said Tortoise.

Now, Tortoise knew that every morning the Hippo family went down to the river to drink. So the next day he half buried himself in the sand right in the path that the Hippos would take. Hippo, his wife and child came down to the river as usual. But suddenly Hippo tripped over Tortoise's shell. 'Oh Instantim! Have you hurt yourself?' his wife asked. So Tortoise heard the secret name.

At the next feast Hippo asked, 'Has anyone discovered my name?'

'Yes!' said Tortoise. 'Your name is Instantim.'

The animals began to eat the feast. And Hippo did as he had said. He took his family down to the river and they have lived in the water from that day to this.

In the old days Thunder and Lightning lived on the earth. But the King made them live at the far end of the town, as far as possible from the other people's houses. Thunder was an old mother sheep, and Lightning was her son – a ram. Whenever the ram got angry he used to burn houses and knock down trees. 'Stop! Stop!' called his mother in a loud, deep voice. But Lightning took no notice.

At last the people could stand it no longer and they complained to the King. So the King said to Thunder and Lightning, 'Go and live in the sky. There you will not do so much harm.' So Thunder and Lightning went to live in the sky. And there they have remained.

Lightning was very angry to be banished. Before he left he knocked down the doors of all the houses in the town. One of those doors belonged to Mouse. It was so old it broke easily, and all the stories on earth ran out.

After that they never went back to dwell with Mouse any more, but remained running up and down all over the earth.

*The myth of Mouse and her story children comes from the Ekoi people of Nigeria. The sources of the other five stories that I have woven in are listed below.*

*Efik Ibibio*
Why the Sun and Moon Live in the Sky
*Ekoi*
How All Animals Came on Earth
*Efik Ibibio*
Why the Hippo Lives in Water
*Yoruba*
Rubber Girl
*Efik Ibibio*
The Story of Lightning and Thunder

*Copyright* © Joanna Troughton 1989
*First published in 1989 by*
Blackie and Son Limited,
7 Leicester Place, London WC2H 7BP

British Library Cataloguing in Publication Data
Troughton, Joanna, *1947-*
  How stories came into the world.
  1. Title
  823'.914[J]

  ISBN 0-216-92605-X

*Designed by* Malcolm Smythe

*Typeset in Cheltenham Light by*
Artworkers Typesetters, London

Printed in Hong Kong

*First American edition
published in 1990 by*
Peter Bedrick Books
2112 Broadway, New York, NY 100203

Library of Congress Cataloging-in-Publication Data
Troughton, Joanna.
  How stories came into the world: a folk tale from west Africa /
retold and illustrated by Joanna Troughton – 1st American ed.
    p. cm. – (Folk tales of the world)
  Summary: Once only Mouse knew, and kept to himself, the stories of
how the world came to be until angry Lightning broke down Mouse's
door and the stories escaped into the world.
  ISBN 0-87226-411-4
  [1. MICE – Folklore.   2. Folklore – Africa, West.]   I. Title.
II. Series: Folk tales of the world (New York, N.Y.)
PZ8.1.T74Ho 1989
398.2' 45293233 – dc19                    88-32159